RAYDALE DOWER
ROBERT ORCHARDSON
FIONA JARDINE
LUCY MCKENZIE
ALAN MICHAEL
CLARE STEPHENSON
ELLEN MUNRO
GRAHAM LITTLE
KATY DOVE
ANDY WAKE
LUKE FOWLER
DUNCAN MARQUISS
KEVIN HUTCHESON
SCOTT MYLES
STEVEN CAIRNS
STEPHEN SUTCLIFFE
THE LONELY PIPER

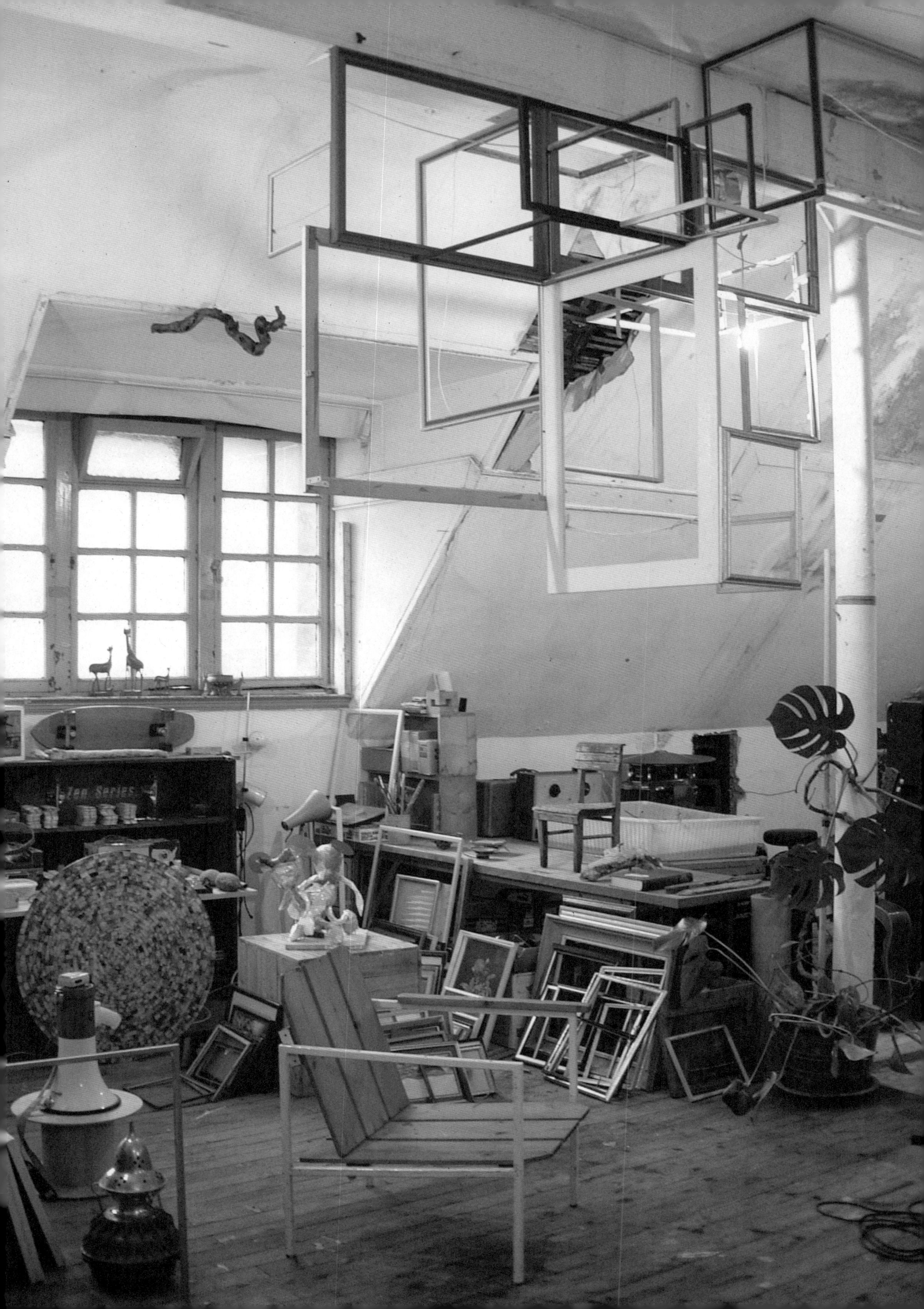

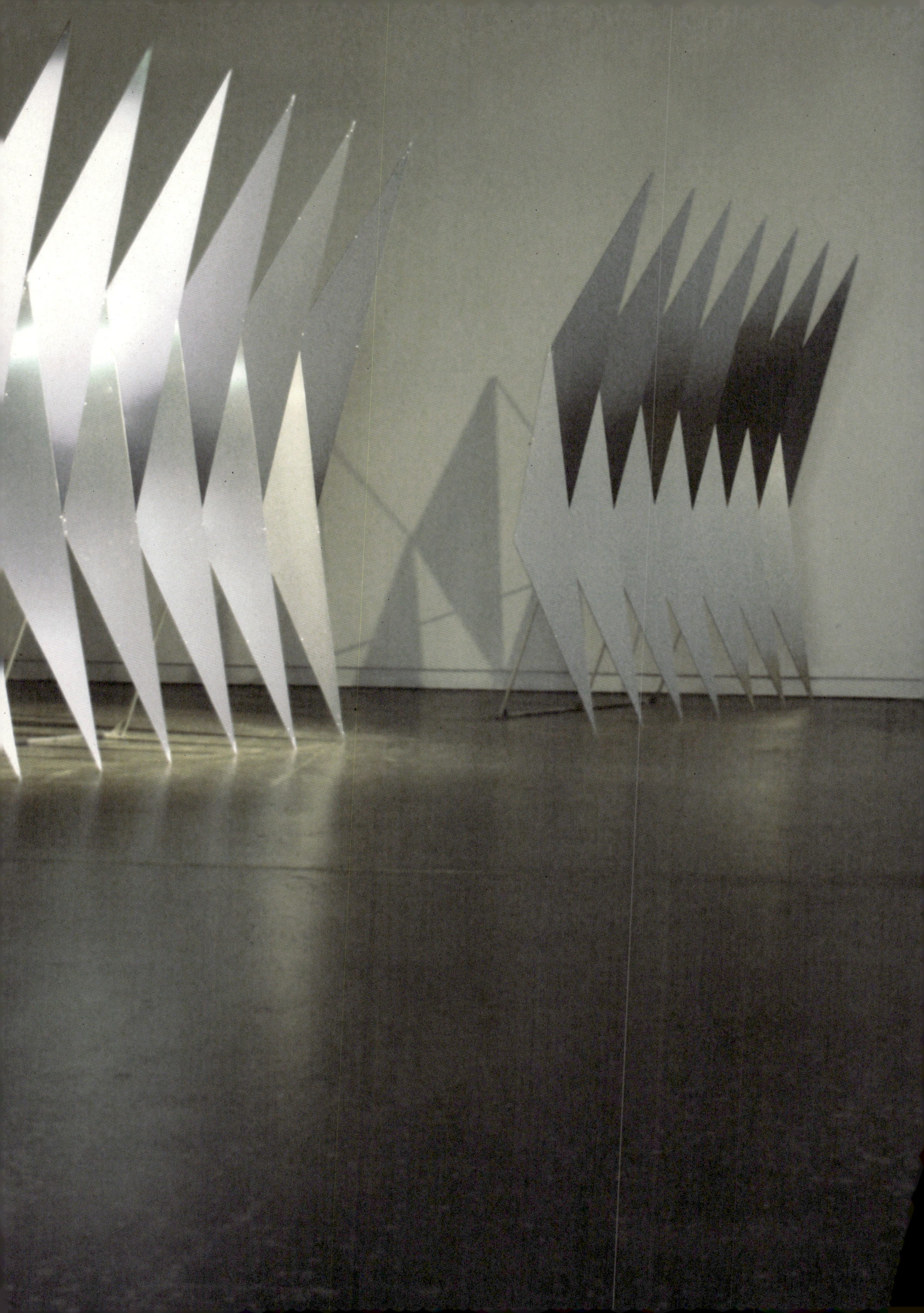

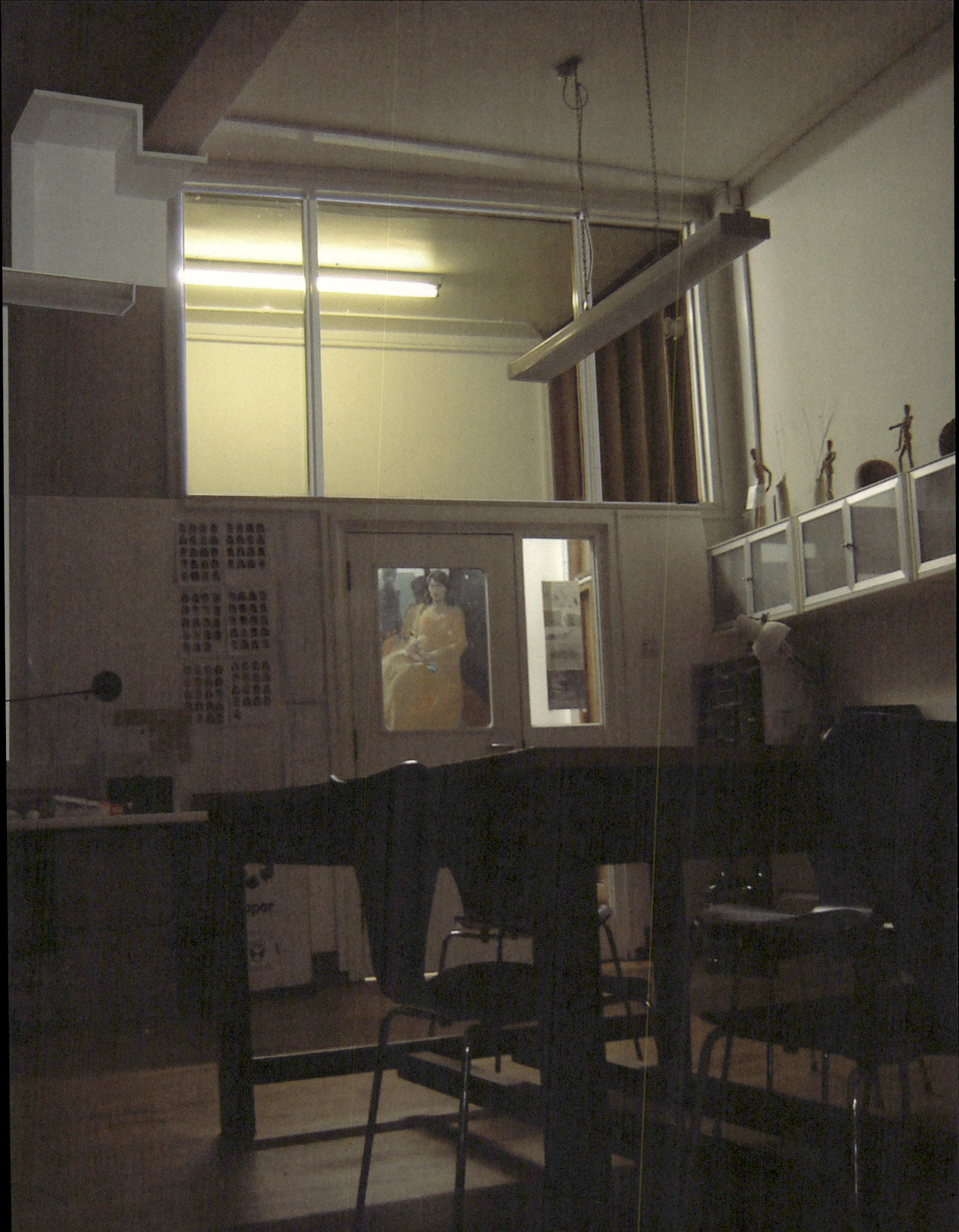

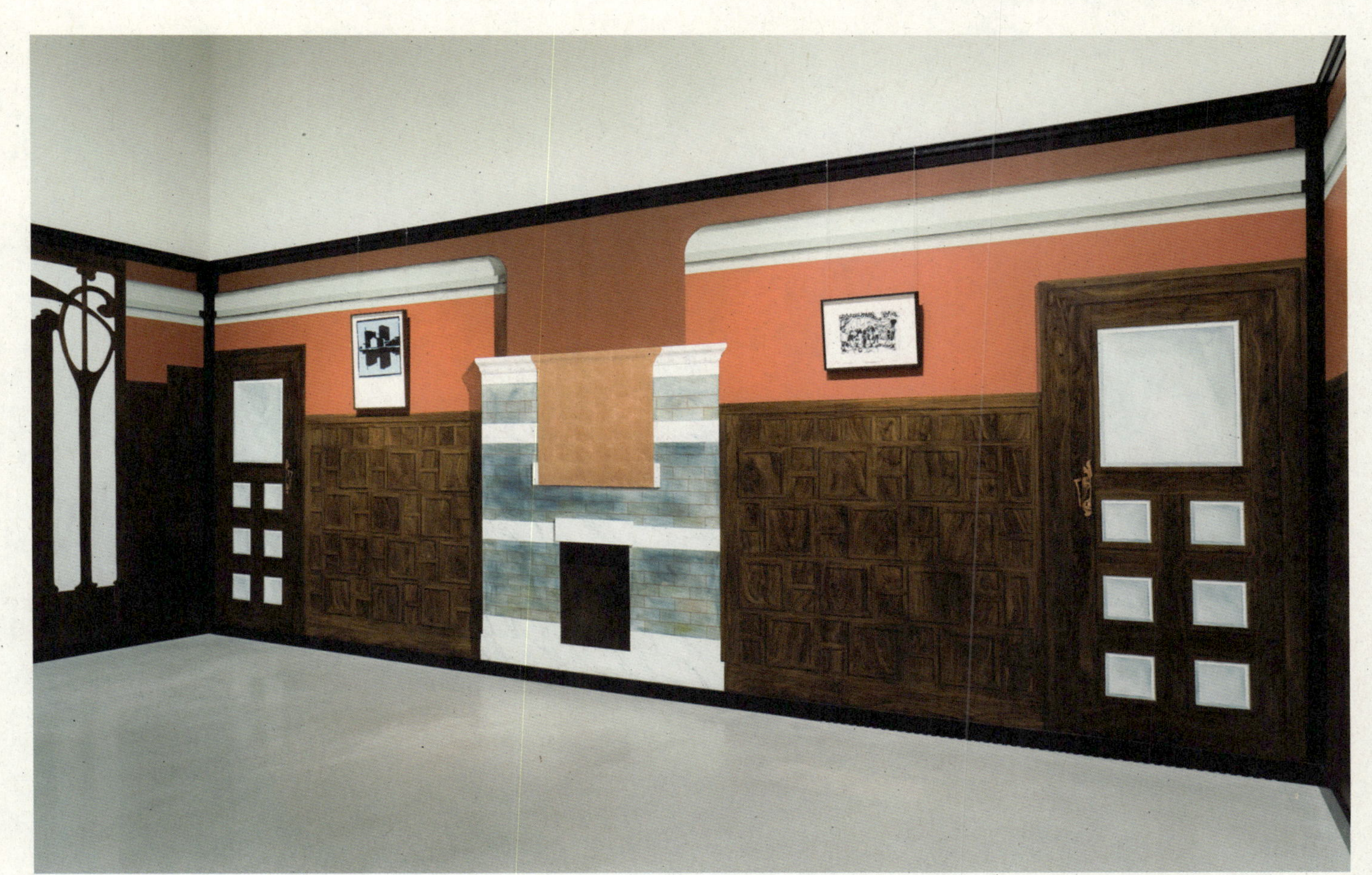

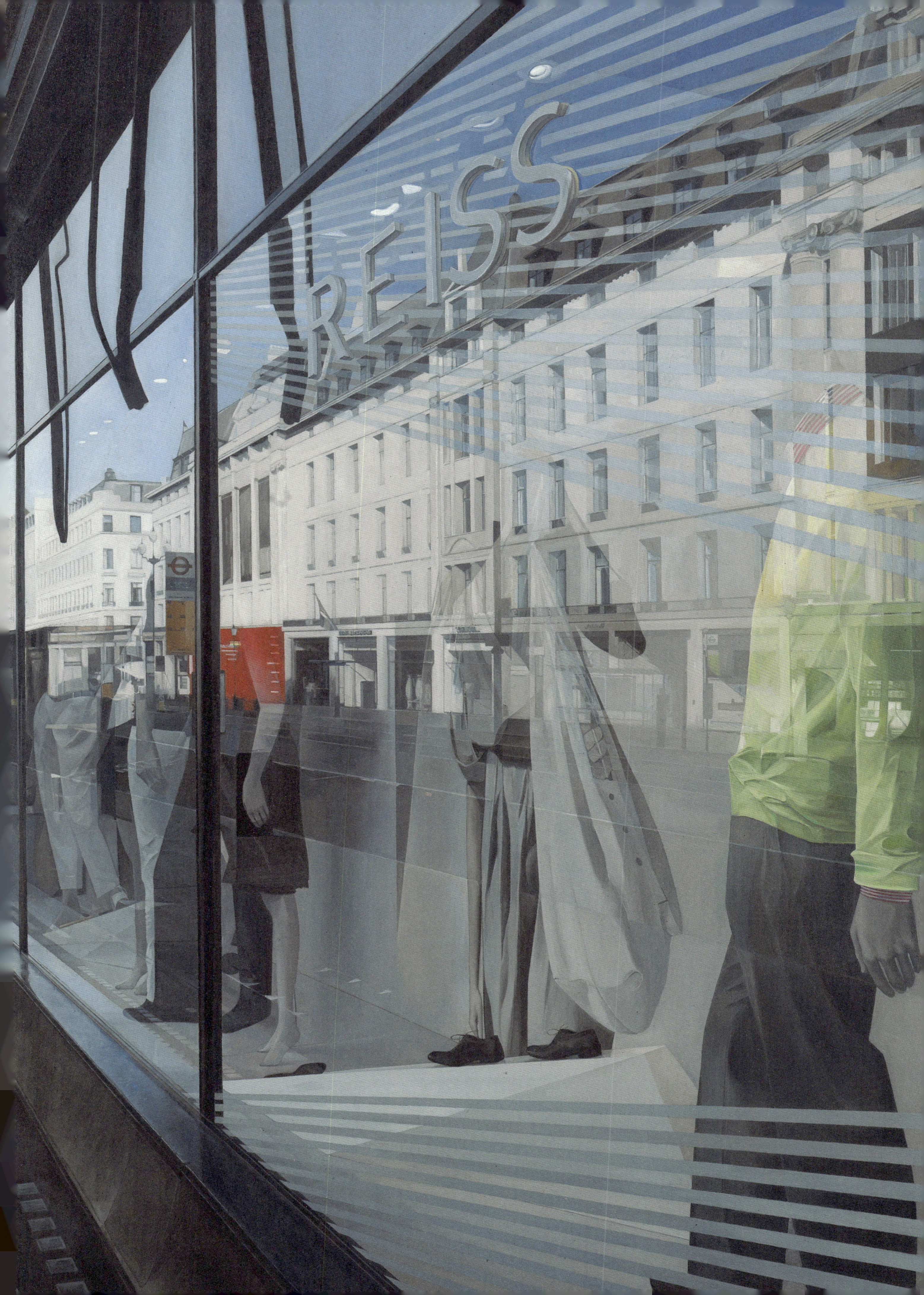

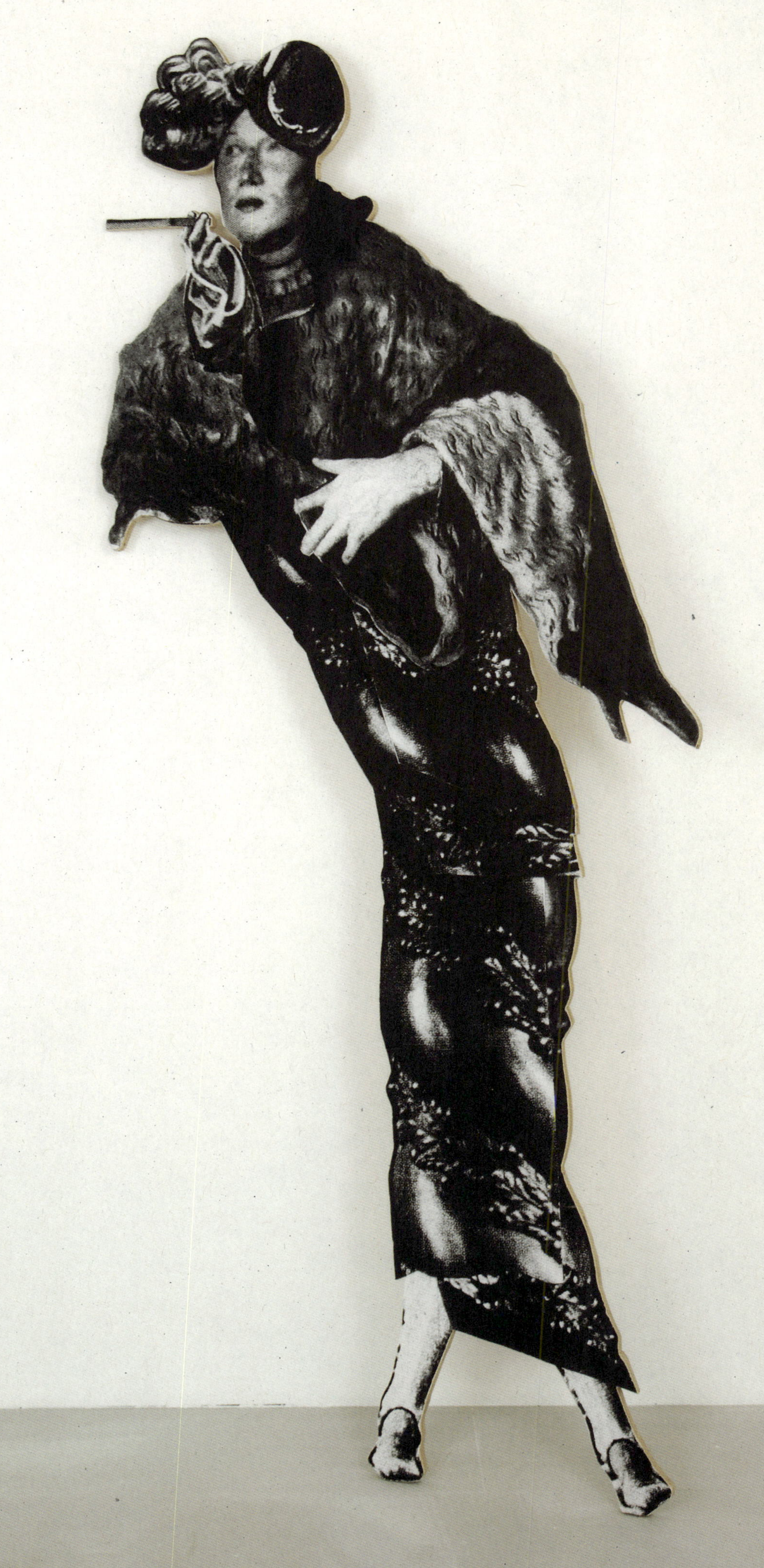

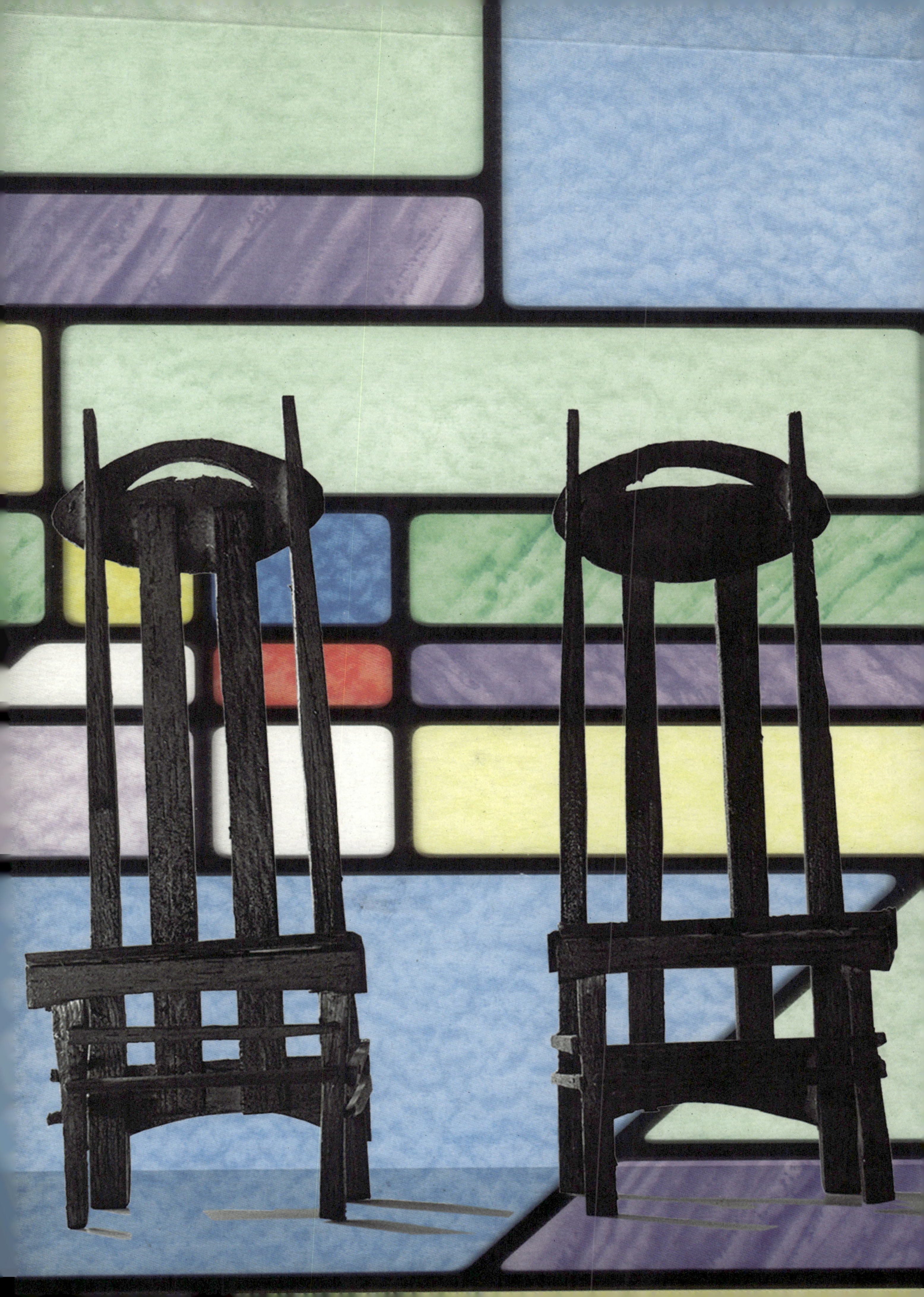

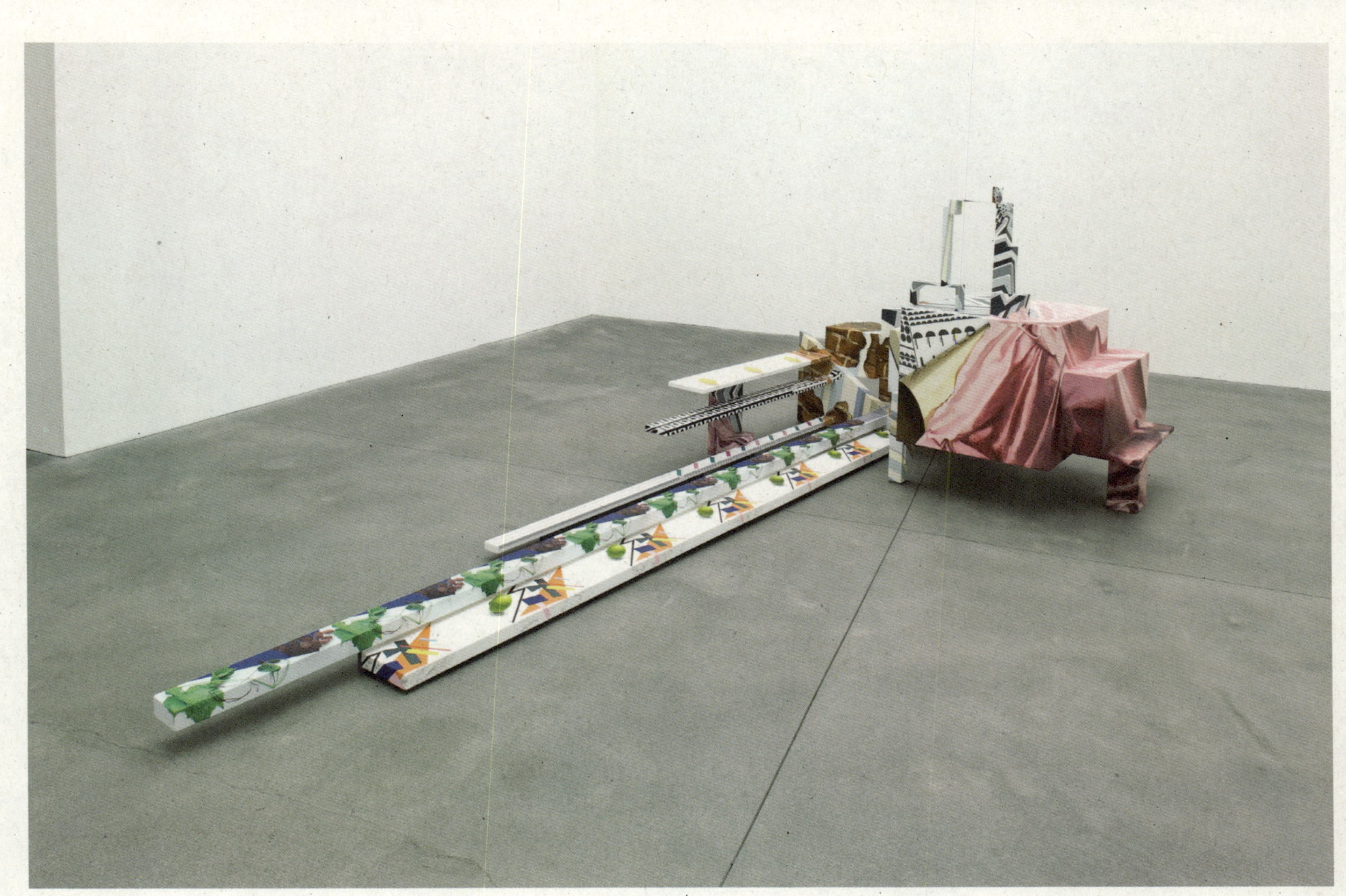

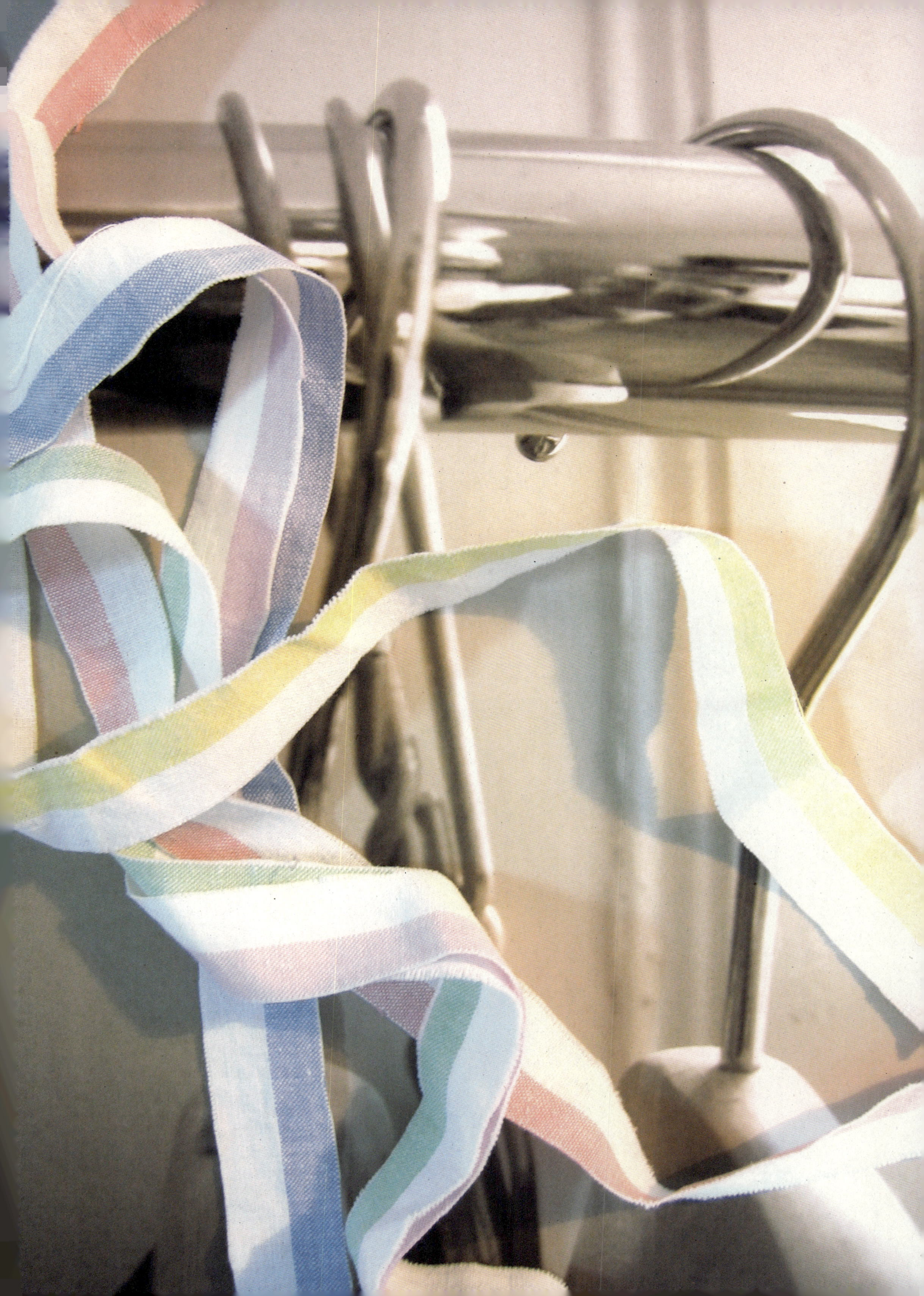

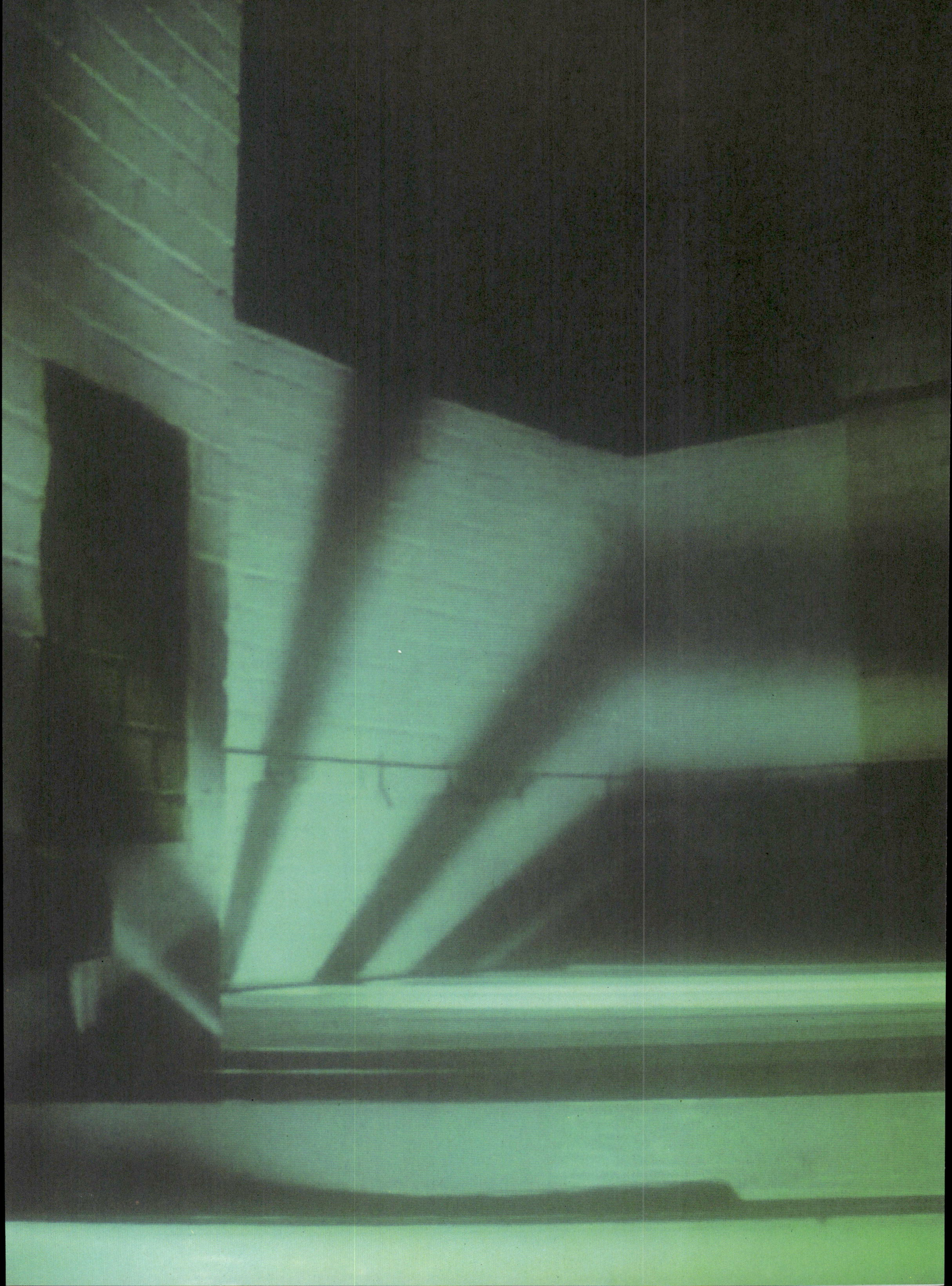

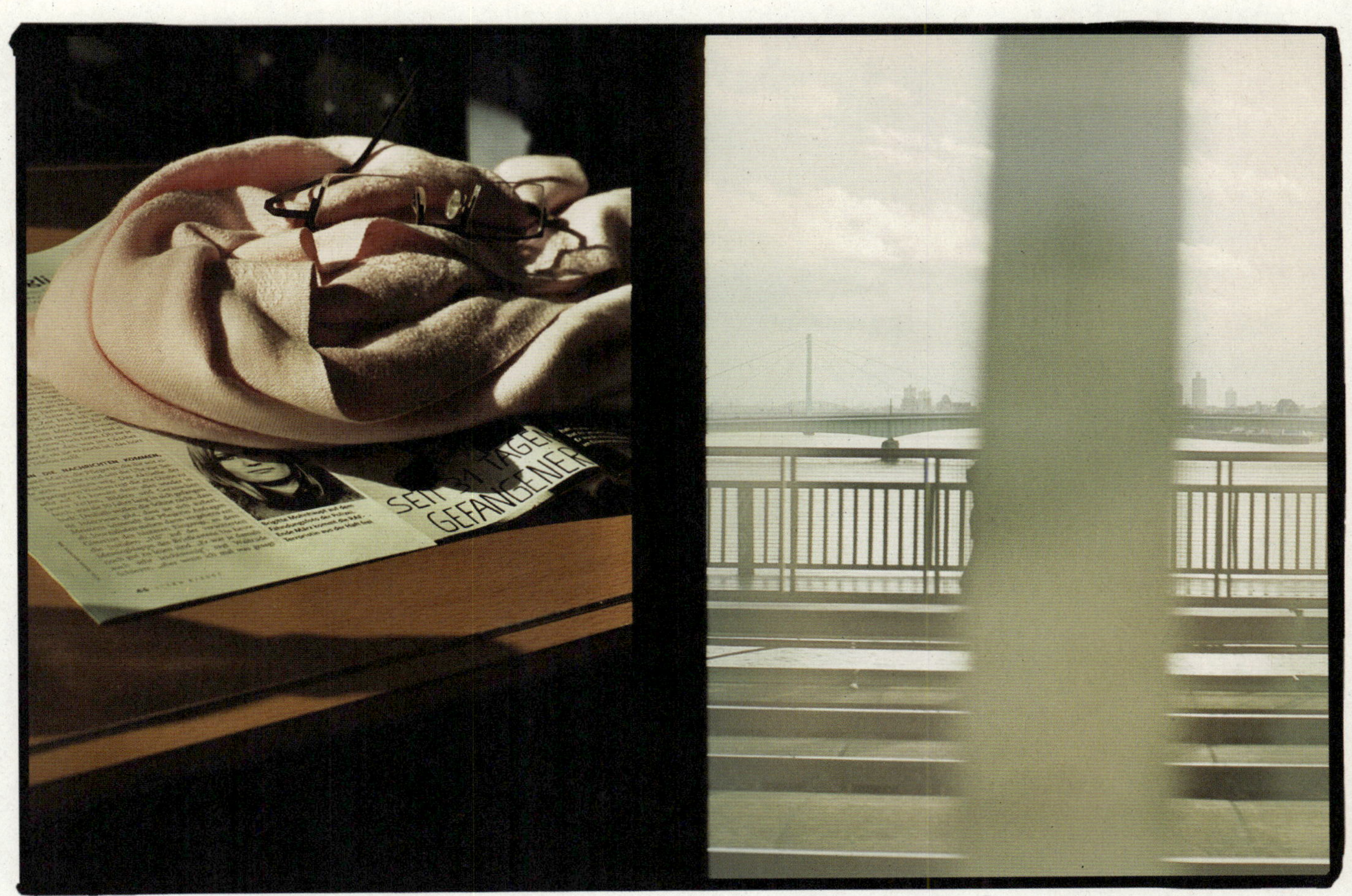
SEIT 31 TAGEN
GEFANGENER

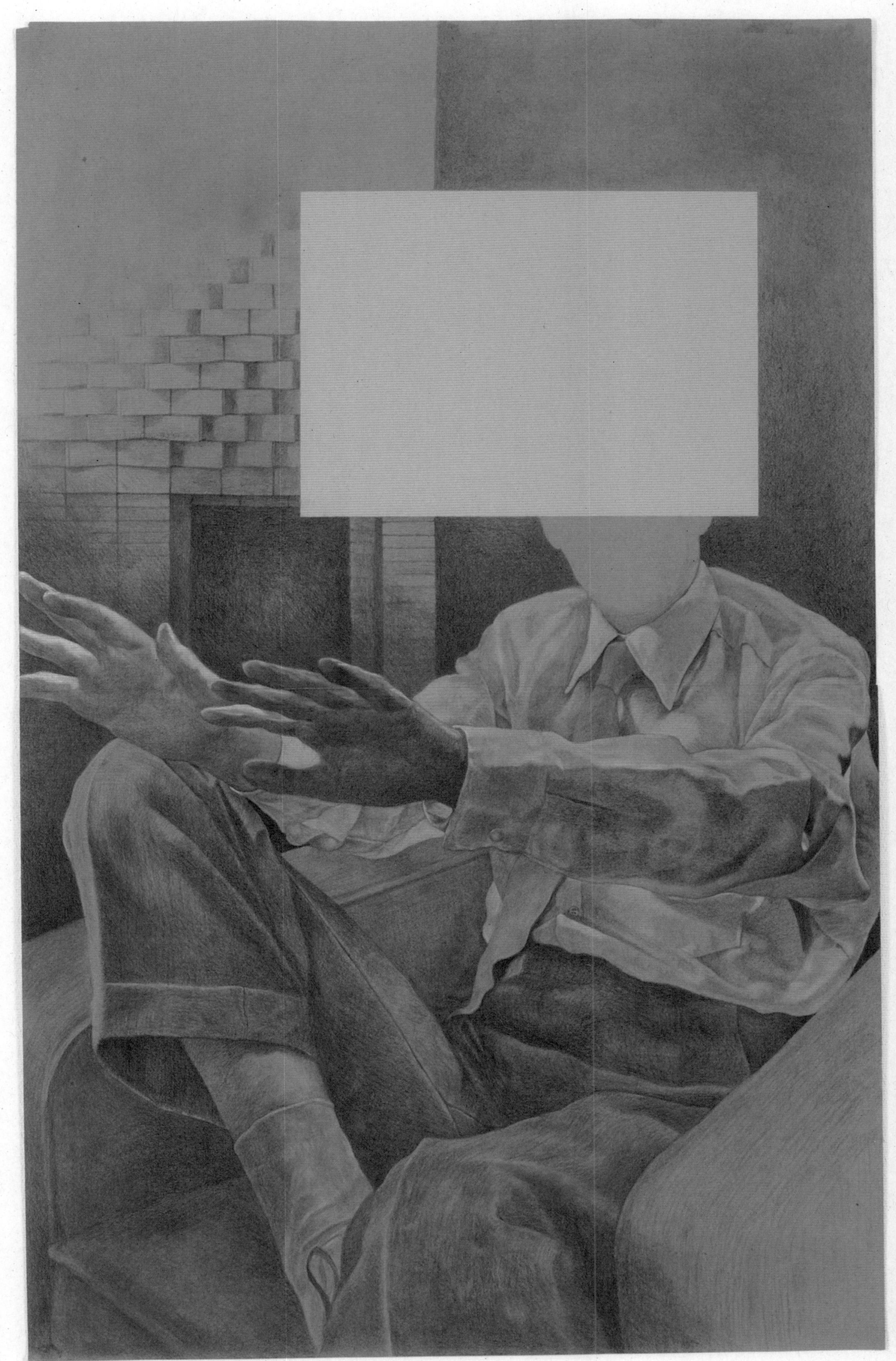

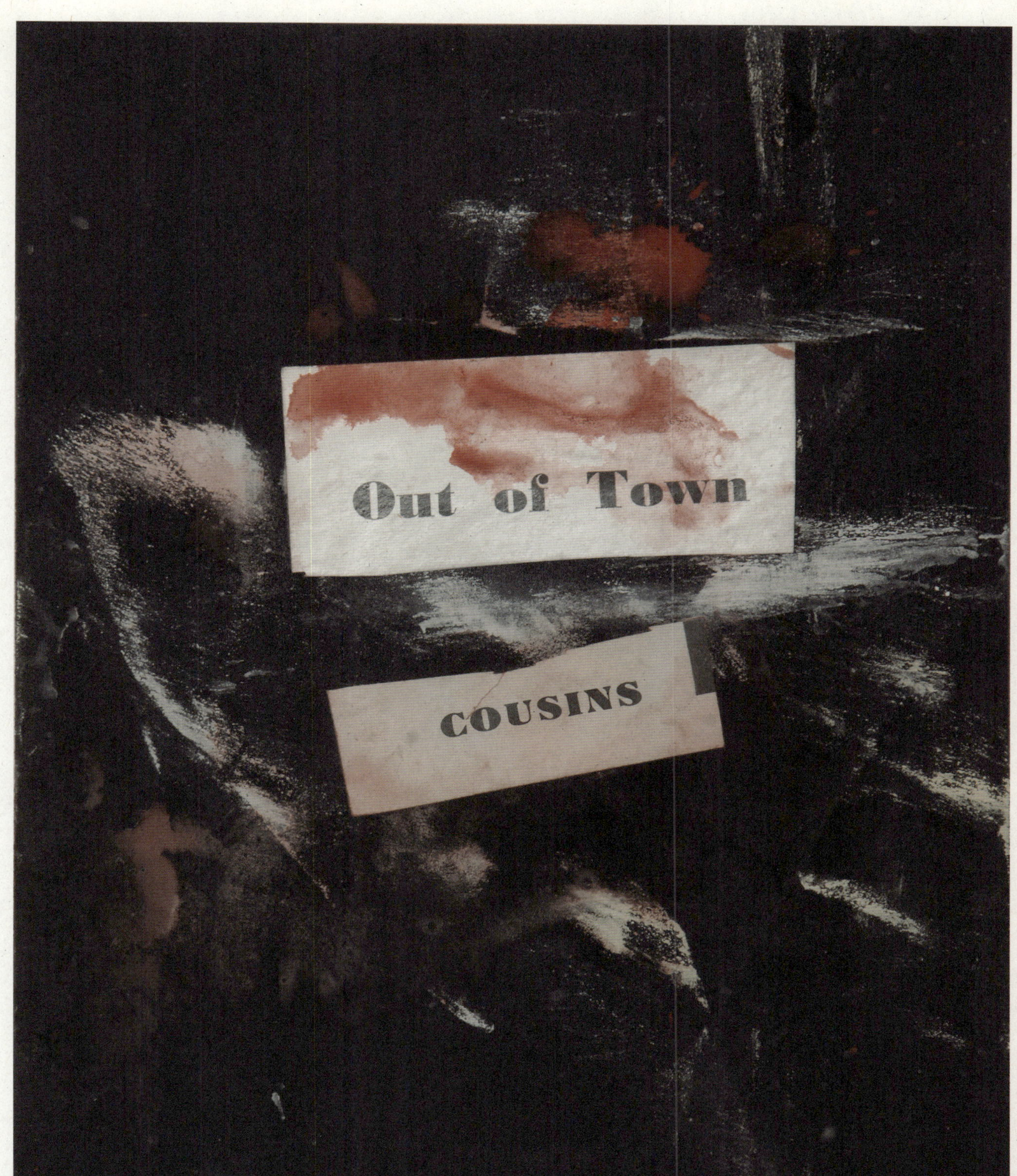
Out of Town
COUSINS

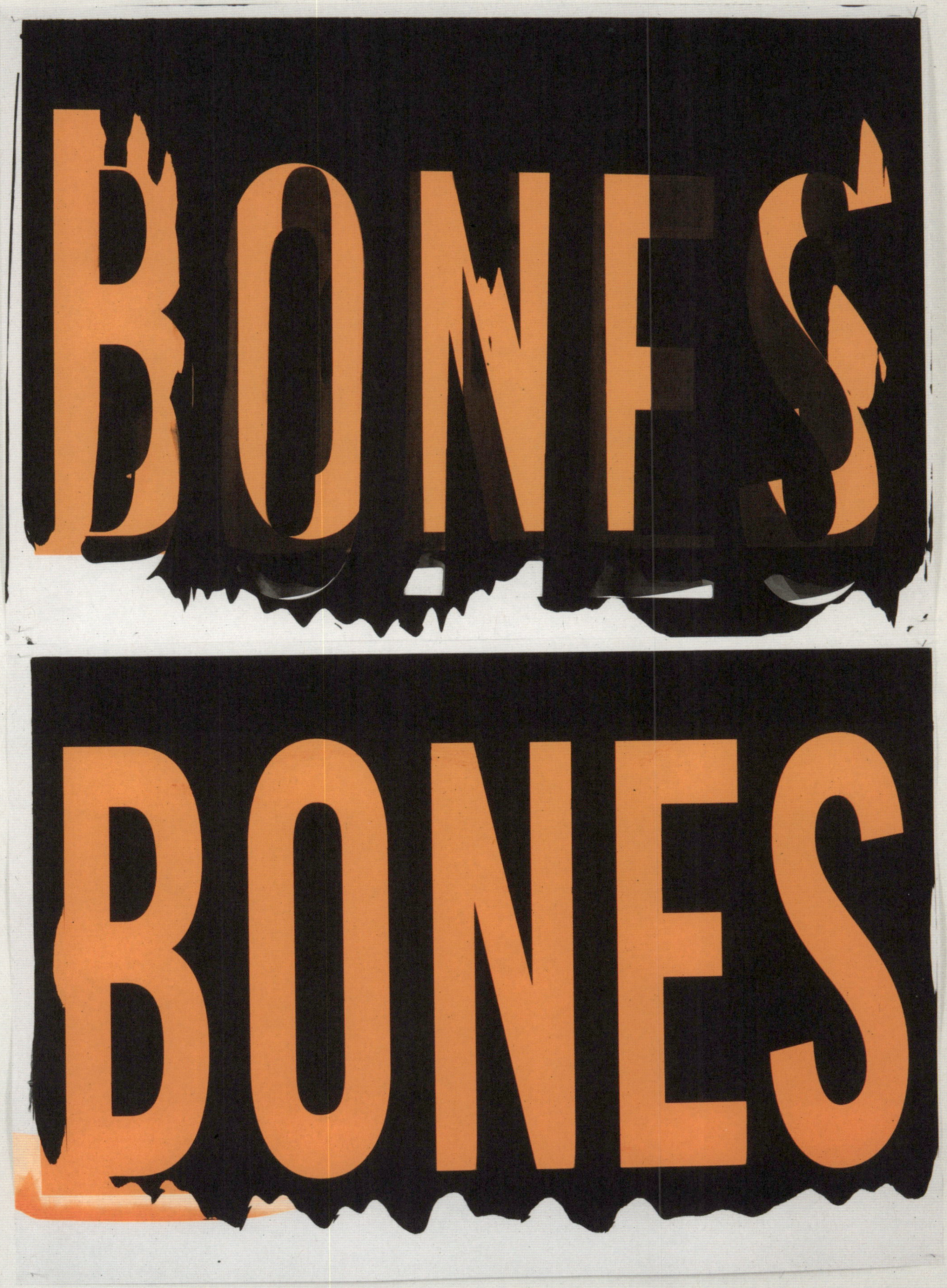

BONES
BONES

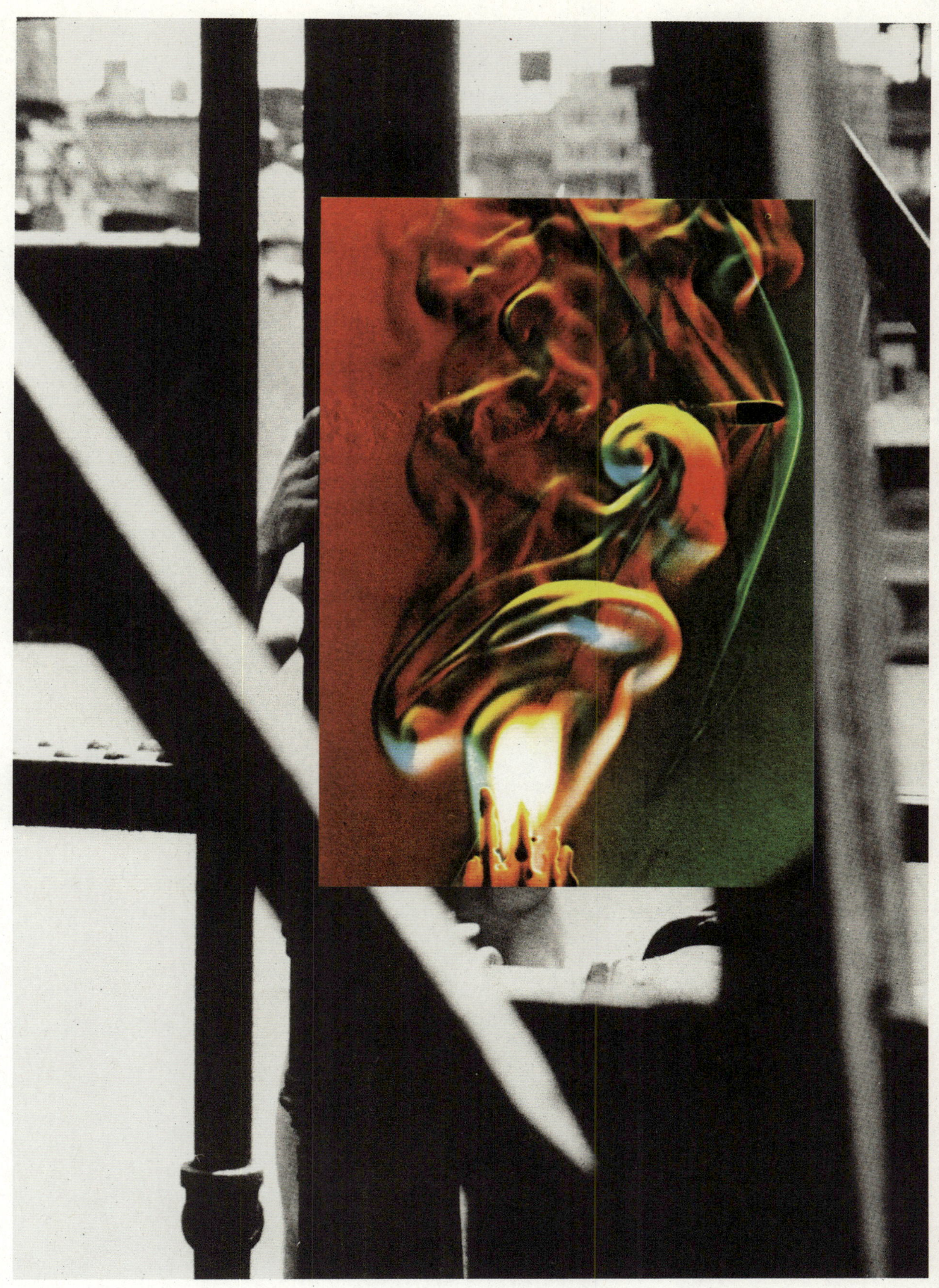

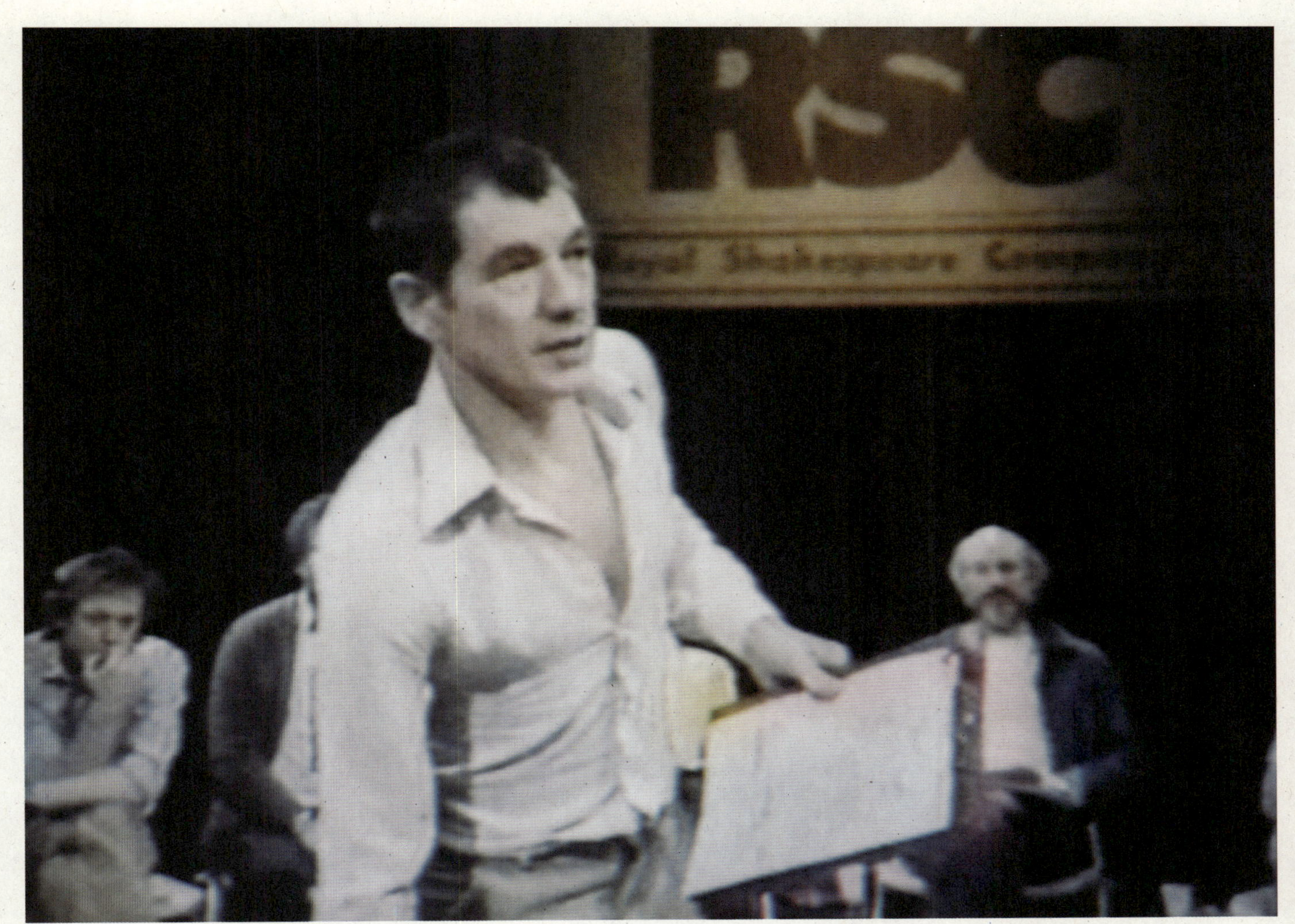
RSC
Royal Shakespeare Company

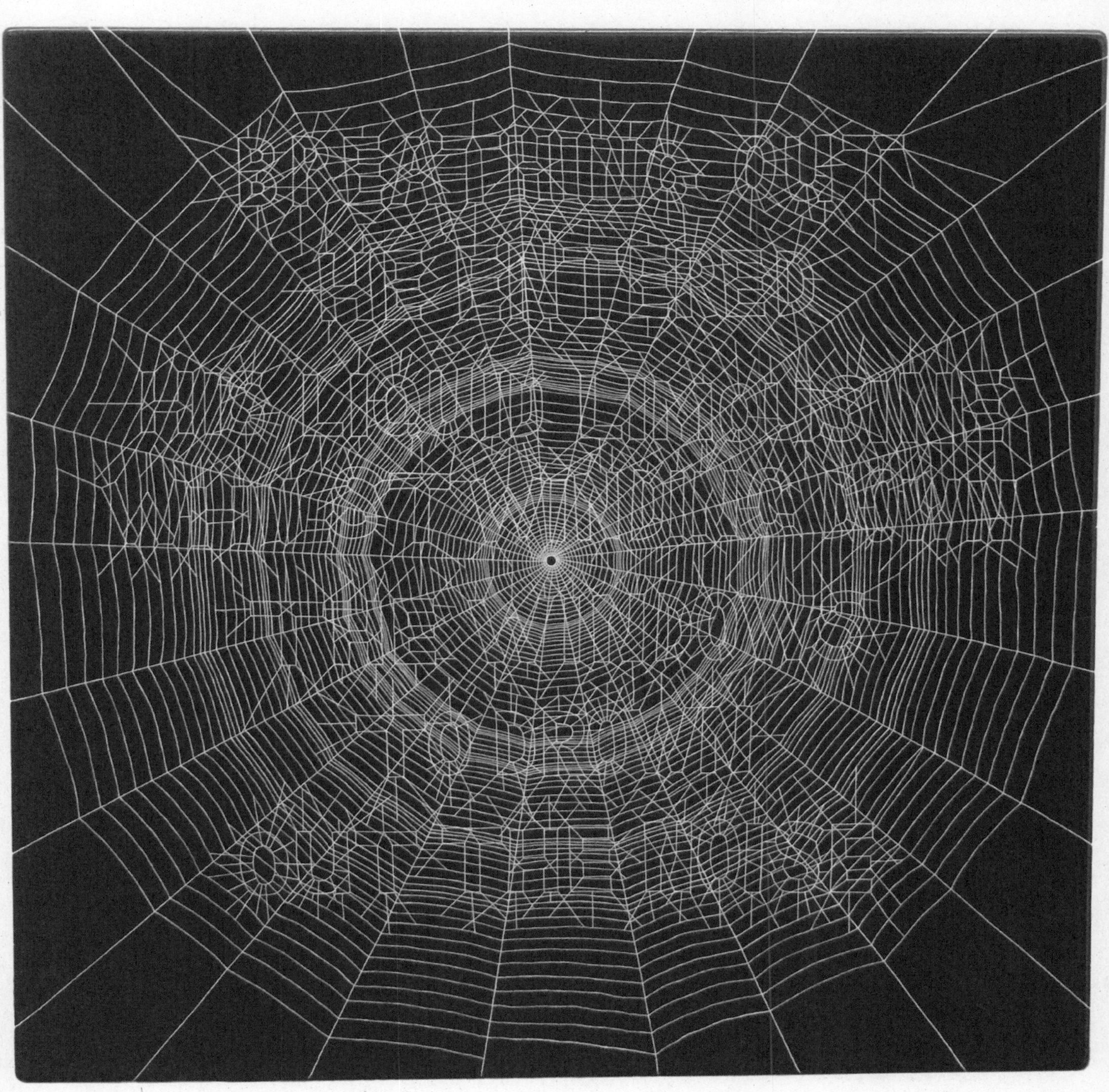

BREATHING OUT
TO DROWN
OUT THE NOISE

<u>FAME AND THE FISHERMAN</u>

A cautionary tale regaled, concerning a quite wonderful actor best described as a kind of 'Robert Burns Downey Jr' character, a peerless yet latterly troubled individual who finds himself returning to his Central Highland homeland, not under duress but under his own volition, to fish his way back to good health (both mental and physical) on the fondly remembered river of his childhood. Escaping (at last) from the latterly shallow running waters of Hollywood; shallow waters up which, his salmon now refuses to run, dammed by tabloid torment and a latter madness in his acting method. Flynn'ed out and creatively hindered, he wisely decides to disembark from his decidedly unstable Tinseltown pedestal.

A few months hence and he finds himself standing alone amidst a sylvan idyll undisturbed, stalking his river's beat with steady heronesques, silently Spey-Casting a blue charm into an ancestral salmon lie (recommended to him by his father). An autumnal sun reflects quite tranquilly off the rivers mirrored surface, benevolently illuminating his periphery with a disco-balled glister. Something within this scene turns like a key, unlocking the doors of his perception, the glittering river becomes in an instant a sparkling simulacrum of camera flash, an illusory interruption to his recuperative reverie. The surrounding flashes dazzle him into a cruelly remembered disorientation; his reviled paparazzi shadow have tracked him down, all the way from LA to the auspicious Tay. The river changes, its purpose reverses, becoming (in his hallucinating head) a chauffeur driven vehicular respite; an imagined door opens within the peat darkened depths and he foolishly steps in, to be (accidentally) ferried away from his troubles and his life by the relentless movement of meltwater and rainfall. He goes with the flow, from fame to flotsam; and is water borne into a legendary realm.

<u>The Lonely Piper 2009</u>

IMAGE CREDITS

RAYDALE DOWER
Artist's studio at 73 Robertson Street, 2009
Photograph for publication, courtesy of the artist.

ROBERT ORCHARDSON
The future is certain, give us time to work it out, 2009
Aluminium, 300cm x 280cm x 80cm, courtesy of the
artist and Wilkinson Gallery, London.

FIONA JARDINE
Untitled, 2009
Photograph for publication, courtesy of the artist.

LUCY MCKENZIE
Installation view, Museum of Modern Art New York, 2008
Courtesy of the artist and Cabinet, London, and Galerie
Daniel Buchholz, Cologne and Berlin.

ALAN MICHAEL
Regent Street, 2008
Oil on canvas, 100 x 76cm, courtesy of the artist
and Stuart Shave/Modern Art, London.

CLARE STEPHENSON
Our-lady-of-the bad-infinity, 2008
Photocopy on plywood, 210cm x 85cm x 2.5cm,
courtesy of the artist and Sorcha Dallas, Glasgow.

ELLEN MUNRO
When east coast girls meet west coast boys, 2009
Collage for publication, courtesy of the artist.

GRAHAM LITTLE
Facts are stupid things (fruit vs fashion), 2007
Plywood, acrylic, gouache, coloured pencil and varnish,
445cm x 180cm x 150cm, courtesy of the artist and
Alison Jacques Gallery, London.

KATY DOVE
Untitled, 2009
Collage for publication, courtesy of the artist
and Hales Gallery, London.

ANDY WAKE
Prefix, 2009
Still from video, courtesy of the artist.

LUKE FOWLER
Photo archive 2006 onwards: Deutsche Bahn, 2006
C–Print, 30 x 45 cm, courtesy of the artist and
The Modern Institute/Toby Webster Ltd, Glasgow.

DUNCAN MARQUISS
Apparent and Unapparent Surfaces, 2008
102cm x 64cm, coloured pencil on paper, courtesy
of the artist and Dicksmith Gallery, London.

KEVIN HUTCHESON
Extended Family, 2008
Magazine cuttings, acrylic, watercolour and household
emulsion on sandpaper, 28 x 23cm, courtesy of the
artist and Jacky Strenz Gallery, Frankfurt.
Photo: Stephen Robinson.

SCOTT MYLES
Bones, 2007
Silkscreen on paper; 2 parts each, 102 x 72 cm,
courtesy of the artist and The Modern Institute/Toby
Webster Ltd, Glasgow. Photo: Ruth Clark.

STEVEN CAIRNS
Untitled (Catch Smoking), 2008
Collage, 25cm x 19cm, courtesy of the artist.

STEPHEN SUTCLIFFE
We'll Let You Know 0:58
Still from video, 2008, courtesy of the artist
and Galerie Micky Schubert, Berlin.

THE LONELY PIPER
Fame and the Fisherman, 2008
Emulsion, pigment and varnish on MDF, 95cm x 95cm,
courtesy of the artist.

City of Disco

The factory was key to my decision to study in Dundee. An empty garage on Perth Road where the DCA now stands it was at one time the only indoor skatepark in Scotland. An autonomous space, the factory was a realisation of the DIY ethos of punk and a lucid illustration of skateboarding's approach to urban space.

More keenly aware of my peers outside of college the underground continued to exert its influence. A new wave of younger tutors from Glasgow encouraged us to experiment with this in approach and subject matter. We organised collaborative exhibitions with the inclusion of performance and music.

Through these shows I made my first contact with Alan Woods who was interested in the Beat spirit of what we were doing. Alan had given a lecture on the Situationist International in a suitably anarchic and disparate style, delivered as he wandered randomly from one idea to another, he introduced the concept of psychogeography and the 'Derive' as a way to negotiate the city.

I recognised in this idea an echo of the way we approached the streets and architecture on skate-boards and he encouraged me to pursue it. Alan also made an impression in the way he wore his trousers: pulled up high like a 30's or 40's Jazz musician, with the waistband nearly in the middle of his chest.

Viva Alan Woods.

Raydale Dower

When I started at Duncan of Jordanstone in 1995, there was less going on in Dundee than there is now. DCA and Generator were yet to exist. We took a DIY approach, organising our own exhibitions and parties. The college was a great support. The exhibitions department sometimes gave us financial assistance to put on exhibitions and we screen-printed our fliers in the printmaking department. We formed an artists group called Unit 13 and organised exhibitions in the derelict cellar of someone's house, a supermarket, a night club and the botanic gardens. Tutors such as Graham Fagen and Cathy Wilkes provided invaluable support and inspiration.

Katy Dove

The first two years at Art College in Dundee I spent hiding under stairwells and behind stacks of chairs. In these hideaways I would construct my own still-lives to draw. I failed my first year. Perhaps I was too self-conscious about my work and would run away from certain projects to the library. The head librarian was always very helpful and would buy just about any exhibition catalogue that I wanted to look at. Somehow those moments spent reading Parkett and Frieze made life as an artist seem more feasible. I would wander through various departments at art college bothering tutors with over enthusiastic questions about material scissors and perspective in architecture. Printed textiles was particularly enticing as it was full of cheery hard-working girls. The overly contemplative Fine Art department consisted of much staring and little work. I sometimes travelled to Edinburgh on the train. These visits would consist of sprints from museum to gallery. I don't remember eating much except once I tried a Scotch Pie and immediately threw up. The most contemporary painting in Dundee then, was a Lord Leighton profile portrait. The lack of easy contact with International Art didn't bother me, rather it intensified my experiences of art elsewhere.

Graham Little

Living in London now, Dundee seems very far away, but I enjoyed my time there. I have heard people talk the city down in the past. I remember hearing Dundee derided for being used as a location for film-makers wanting to shoot somewhere that looked like eastern bloc Europe, but I found this sort of thing actually quite endearing. I miss things about Dundee like the particular sense of community that it fostered. I lived there for almost ten years, and it felt like the art college and wider city underwent quite a change during that time. When I arrived to study, Duncan of Jordanstone felt like it had more of a sense of autonomy from the university, and there was a good mixture of younger as well as more experienced artists teaching there. In the years that followed my graduation, there seemed to be more of a sense of potential in Dundee. DCA opened, Generator began, and former students began staying in the city longer.

Robert Orchardson

Here I sit, Ouija board senseless and quietly concocting some lettered scenarios in the cold comfort of my happily haunted home. Intermittently gazing out of the bay-window of my west end- east-coast crow's nest, on its top of the hill, top of the building elevation, a vantage point from which, I'm able to see sleeping seals from the security of my sitting room; those common and sand-barred commas which languidly mark a mid-Tay pause between here and Fife. And as is the weathers wont, it is clement. These are just a few of the reasons for my remaining here; reasons for which, there are a multitude.

The Lonely Piper

I guess two of the more formative memories I have from the time I spent studying in Dundee are of an individual and an exhibition. The late historian, writer and artist Alan Woods was a tutor whom I learned a great deal from, both through the lectures that he gave, and the frequent informal conversations we would have in my studio, and in the pub. I still have a piece of his work on the wall of my flat. Suburban Affair was an exhibition held in an empty townhouse in Newport-On- Tay in 1997, and included four of the artists who are featured in The Associates. This was the first real show I was in outside of college, while I was still in my final year at Duncan Of Jordanstone, and the peer group I exhibited with back then are artists whom I still call friends, and have since gone on to show with on a number of occasions.

Kevin Hutcheson

We moved to Dundee when I was seven and I went to primary and secondary school on the Perth Road. My school bus would go past the art college and I'd see students coming and going, sitting on the steps and I just wanted to be there too. I remember the first week with Pete Collins he was addressing the class and talking about art and what it meant to make art and the hairs on the back on my neck stood up. He said that if he had his way there'd be two banners on either side of the front entrance, one would say 'Be not afraid' and the other 'Art is Love'. I went on in that class to do a particularly hideous oil of a horse and a wire fence silhouetted against a pastel sky. The words had stuck but they'd yet to sink in.

Ellen Munro

Dundee Contemporary Arts was an old garage on the Perth Road where I used to skateboard. Duncan of Jordanstone offered me access to a brilliant library, some good tutors and a peer group; I was lucky, there were some talented people at Art School while I was studying there, and the College didn't have some overblown legacy to contend with: everything felt possible. We became pro active and organised exhibitions; I've shown

with many of the artists exhibiting in The Associates before. During my first year Hoover were giving away free flights to New York City; I visited with my brother. In third year I went on exchange, then moved to Vancouver upon graduation. Dundee was a good city to study in; it made you look outside.

Scott Myles

Dundee (Scottish Gaelic: Dùn Dèagh) is the fourth-largest city in Scotland and, fully named as Dundee City, one of Scotland's 32 local government council areas. It lies on the north bank of the Firth of Tay, which feeds into the North Sea.

Dundee and the surrounding area has been continuously occupied since the Mesolithic age. The port developed initially on the back of the wool trade exporting wool from the Angus hinterland. Once it was cheaper to produce linen, which had supplanted the wool trade and was itself under pressure from cotton abroad, the weavers turned their skills to weaving imported jute. The weaving industry caused the city to grow rapidly with many migrant workers though the town contained very few stone buildings prior to 1860. In this period, Dundee also gained a reputation for its mar-malade industry and its journalism, giving Dundee its epithet as the city of "jam, jute and journalism".

According to the latest estimates (2006), the population of Dundee City is around 141,930. Dundee's recorded population reached a peak

of 182,204 in the 1971 census, but has since declined due to outward migration.

Today, Dundee is promoted as the City of Discovery, in honour of Dundee's history of scientific activities and of the RRS Discovery, Robert Falcon Scott's Antarctic exploration vessel, which was built in Dundee and is now berthed in the city harbour. Biomedical and technological industries have arrived since the 1980s, and the city now accounts for 10% of the United Kingdom's digital-entertainment industry. Dundee has two universities - the University of Abertay Dundee and the University of Dundee.

Andy Wake

I was thinking recently how strong the art school was in Dundee, I wonder if me and Andy were lucky and caught the tail end of a particular period.

Duncan Marquiss

Dundee land of jazz funk, stovies and all night bakeries. I loved staying in Dundee for the years that I attended art college. I came up with a friend from the portfolio course in Glasgow John Carroll and we soon befriended local lad Derek Lodge, who graciously welcomed us into his fold. There was a great bond between people involved in the local music scene - Mark Wallace and Andy Balneaves and us students. Other kind, funny and influential people I met in Dundee were Steve and Fiona, Katy, Duncan, Mickey, Kevin, Mark, Lucy and Anna, Cathy and Victoria, the late great Alan

Woods, Frank and Egor. In my year I will always remember Michael, Janie, Andy, Duncan, Andy and Duncan (underlings) and Dan (prefect), who I curated a drawing show with in the college.

I recall one day in first year encountering a very alien sight – a funeral procession of some of the most finely dressed, aging rock stars I've ever seen, mixed with a bunch of Dundee folks entering the local church (next to DCA). My older, more savvy, flatmate John realised that it was Billy MacKenzie's funeral procession; it was the first time I'd heard of the Associates.

Luke Fowler

BIOGRAPHIES

Raydale Dower was born in Aberdeen in 1973 and graduated from DJCAD in 1997. An artist and musician (Tut VuVu and Uncle John and Whitelock), exhibitions include The Secret Agent, Glasgow International at Low Salt, and projects at The Custard Factory, Birmingham; The Changing Room, Stirling and Catalyst Arts, Belfast. Raydale will undertake a Creative Lab residency at the Centre for Contemporary Arts, Glasgow in November. Dower lives and works in Glasgow.

———

Robert Orchardson was born in Glasgow in 1976. He attained his BA (Hons) from DJCAD in 1998 and a PG Dip in Fine Art from Goldsmiths College, London in 2004. Recent exhibitions include Galerie Ben Kaufmann, Berlin; Generator Projects, Dundee; The Centre for Contemporary Arts, Glasgow; The International Project Space, Birmingham and Rowley Kennerk Gallery, Chicago. Robert lives and works in London. He is represented by Wilkinson Gallery, London.

———

Born in Galashiels in 1970, Fiona Jardine gained her undergraduate degree from DJCAD in 1998 and an MFA from Glasgow School of Art in 2003. A former committee member of Generator Projects, Dundee, Jardine has exhibited in group exhibitions at Transmission; Centre d'Art Mira Phalaina/Maison Poulaire, Montreuil, France; Tramway Glasgow; The Changing Room, Stirling and solo exhibitions at Sorcha Dallas, Glasgow and Nought to Sixty, ICA, London. Jardine lives in Glasgow and teaches at Duncan of Jordanstone College of Art and Design, Dundee.

———

Lucy McKenzie was born in Glasgow in 1977. Lucy graduated from DJCAD in 1999 and in 2008 completed a course of traditional study at the Van Der Kelen Institute for decorative painting in Brussels. Recent exhibitions include The Musum of Modern Art, New York; SFMoMA, San Francisco; Arnolfini, Bristol; Talbot Rice Gallery, Edinburgh; The Norwich Gallery, Norwich and The Lighthouse Centre, Glasgow and has a forthcoming solo exhibition at The Ludwig Museum, Cologne. Lucy lives and works in Brussels. She is represented by Cabinet, London and Galerie Daniel Buchholz, Cologne and Berlin.

———

Born in Glasgow in 1967, Alan Michael graduated from the MFA at Glasgow School of Art in 1998 having gained a BA (Hons) in Fine Art from DJCAD in 1996. Recent solo exhibitions include Art Now at Tate Britain; Talbot Rice Gallery, Edinburgh and David Kordansky, Los Angeles, and group exhibitions at Galerie Guido W Baudach, Berlin and Modern Art, London. Alan Michael lives and works in Glasgow. He is represented by Sorcha Dallas, Glasgow and Stuart Shave/Modern Art, London.

———

Born in Newcastle-Upon-Tyne in 1972, Clare Stephenson graduated from DJCAD in 1996 before serving on Glasgow's Transmission Gallery committee. Stephenson has exhibited in group shows in Glasgow, Edinburgh, Stirling, Dundee, London, Berlin, Milan and New York and in solo exhibitions at Edinburgh's Talbot Rice Gallery; Dicksmith, London; Sorcha Dallas, Glasgow and Linn Lühn, Cologne and in the two person exhibition The Dirty Hands at the Centre for Contemporary Arts, Glasgow with Alex Pollard. Stephenson lives and works in Glasgow. She is represented by Sorcha Dallas, Glasgow.

———

Ellen Munro was born in Stirling in 1980 and went to school in Dundee. Ellen graduated from DJCAD in 2002 with a BA (Hons) in Printmaking and an MFA in painting from Edinburgh College of Art in 2004. Exhibitions include Market Gallery, Glasgow, The Changing Room, Stirling, The Talbot Rice Gallery, Edinburgh, Generator Projects, Dundee and Young Athenians at The Royal Scottish Academy, Edinburgh and The Athens Biennial. Munro is on the board of the Collective Gallery, Edinburgh. Ellen lives and works in Edinburgh.

———

Graham Little was born in Glasgow in 1972 and went to school in Dundee, he graduated from DJCAD in 1995 and from Goldsmith's College, London with an MA in Fine Art in 1997. Exhibitions include Alison Jacques Gallery, London, The Mizuma Art Gallery, Tokyo, Galerie Max Hetzler, Berlin and The Camden Arts Centre, London. Graham lives and works in London. He is represented by Alison Jacques Gallery, London.

———

Katy Dove was born in Oxford in 1970. Katy graduated from DJCAD in 1999. Recent solo projects include Artis, Den Bosch, The Netherlands; Talbot Rice Gallery, Edinburgh; Pump House Gallery, London; Sies and Hoeke Gallerie, Dusseldorf and Tramway, Glasgow (with Victoria Morton). Katy has a forthcoming collaborative project with Simon Yuill at The Changing Room, Stirling. Katy is a member of the eight piece group Muscles of Joy. She lives and works in Glasgow. Dove is represented by Hales Gallery, London.

———

Andy Wake was born in Dundee in 1978. He graduated in 2001 with a BA (Hons) and in 2006 with an MA from DJCAD. Exhibitions include Nought to Sixty at the ICA, London; New Work Scotland at the Collective Gallery, Edinburgh; Arnolfini, Bristol; The Embassy, Edinburgh and S1 Artspace, Sheffield. Andy is also a musician and is a member of The Phantom Band and Omnivore Demon. He lives and works in Dundee and Glasgow.

———

Luke Fowler was born in Glasgow in 1978. He graduated from DJCAD in 2000. He has exhibited recently at Kunshalle, Zurich; Esther Schipper, Berlin; The Modern Institute/Toby Webster Ltd, Glasgow and has a forthcoming solo exhibition at The Serpentine, London. Screenings of his films include The Edinburgh Film Festival, Edinburgh and Kill Your Timid Notion at DCA. Luke was awarded the prestigious Jarman award for artist film-makers in 2008. Fowler lives and works in Glasgow. He is represented by The Modern Institute/Toby Webster Ltd, Glasgow.

———

Born in Dumfries in 1979, Duncan Marquiss graduated from Printmaking in 2001 at DJCAD and from the MFA at Glasgow School of Art in 2005. Solo exhibitions include The Changing Room, Stirling and Dicksmith Gallery, London. Group exhibitions include Where the Wild Things Are at DCA and also Jack Hanley, San Francisco; The Embassy Gallery Edinburgh and Zenomap, the Scottish Pavilion at the Venice Biennale in 2003. Duncan is also a musician and is a member of The Phantom Band and Omnivore Demon. He lives and works in London and Glasgow. Marquiss is represented by Dicksmith Gallery, London.

———

Kevin Hutcheson was born in Glasgow in 1971. Kevin graduated from DJCAD in 1997 and from an MA in Fine Art from Chelsea College of Art and Design in 2002. He has recently presented solo exhibitions at Galerie Jacky Strenz, Frankfurt and Alexandre Pollazzon, London. Recent group exhibitions include Learn To Read, Tate Modern, London; East International, Norwich Gallery, Norwich and Country Grammar, Gallery of Modern Art, Glasgow. Hutcheson lives and works in Glasgow. He is represented by Galerie Jacky Strenz, Frankfurt.

———

Scott Myles was born in Dundee in 1975 and trained at DJCAD in 1997. Scott lives and works in Glasgow. Recent exhibitions include The Scottish National Gallery of Modern Art, Edinburgh, Meyer Riegger, Karlsruhe, The Breeder, Athens, The Modern Institute, Glasgow and Sadie Coles HQ, London and Kunsthalle, Zurich. Scott was also included in the 2006 Tate Triennial, Tate Britain, London. Scott lives and works in Glasgow. He is represented by The Modern Institute/Toby Webster Ltd, Glasgow.

———

Steven Cairns was born in Kirkcaldy, Fife in 1983. He graduated from in 2005 with a BA (hons) and in 2006 with an MA from DJCAD. Recent exhibitions include the The Gothenburg Biennal, Sweden in 2007 and They Had Four Years at Generator Projects, Dundee in 2006. Steven lives and works in Dundee.

———

Stephen Sutcliffe was born in Harrogate in 1968. He graduated from DJCAD in 1998 and received an MFA from Glasgow School of Art. Stephen is a former committee member of Generator Projects. Recent exhibitions of his work include Nought to Sixty at the ICA, London; Gaudel de Stampa, Paris; Art Now, Tate Britain, London; The Centre for Contemporary Art, Glasgow; Hotel, London and Tart Contemporary, San Francisco. Stephen lives and works in Glasgow. Sutcliffe is represented by Galerie Micky Schubert, Berlin.

———

The Lonely Piper (C.R.M born in 1975, Inverness / T.L.P born 1999, Rannoch Moor) graduated in 1998 from DJCAD. Selected recent group exhibitions include The Bloomberg Space, London; Textual Healing, The Embassy Gallery, Edinburgh; Where The Wild Things Are, DCA; Campbell's Soup, Glasgow School of Art; Albatross, Galeria Sztuki, Wozownia, Poland. The Lonely Piper lives and works in Dundee.

———